DUEL OF THE IRONCLADS

THE MONITOR VS. THE VIRGINIA

PATRICK O'BRIEN

WALKER & COMPANY ✦ NEW YORK

Huge waves washed over the *Monitor*'s deck and smashed against the turret. Tons of seawater poured into the little iron ship. Desperate sailors leaped into the lifeboats of a nearby navy steamship and were rowed to safety as the *Monitor* dove through the waves. But when a boat returned to rescue the rest of the men, the *Monitor* was gone.

The storm had done what the enemy couldn't do. The *Monitor* would fight no more. It had been built less than a year before but had become the most famous warship in the world. Its battle with the ironclad *Virginia*, sometimes called the *Merrimack*, had shown the world the power of iron. It was a completely new kind of ship. No one had ever seen anything like it.

For hundreds of years before the *Monitor*, ships of war were built of wood and were powered by the wind. Their sides bristled with cannons.

In battle, warships blasted away at each other with heavy iron cannonballs, trying to bash in the wooden sides of the enemy ship and knock down the wooden masts. The ship with the most cannons almost always won.

In the early 1800s, shipbuilders in England and France started attaching plates of iron to the wooden sides of warships. A ship that was clad in iron should be protected from the enemy's cannon-balls. But this idea had not yet been tested in battle.

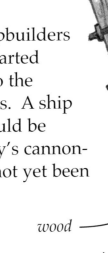

wood —

iron —

It was not an entirely new idea. About 250 years earlier, the Koreans had built "turtle ships." An iron lid protected the warriors inside.

At about the same time, shipbuilders were building steam engines into sailing ships. A ship powered only by sails had to wait for a good wind before it could go anywhere. But with steam power added, a ship could travel even when there was no wind.

The first "ironclad" in the world was the French La Gloire. It was powered by sail and steam.

In America, the states in the southeastern part of the country weren't happy with the government in Washington, D.C. In 1861, the Southern states decided that they no longer wanted to be a part of the United States. They formed their own country and called it the Confederate States of America.

President Abraham Lincoln did not want to see the Union of states, the United States, broken up. So the Northern Union and the Southern Confederates went to war. The North and the South would battle each other for four years in the Civil War.

The North had big wooden warships, and it had shipyards to build even more. It had iron foundries for making cannons and factories for making steam engines.

At the beginning of the war the South had a few small warships, but they didn't have the shipyards and factories to build more. They wanted to try out an untested idea, an iron-armored ship. An "ironclad" should be able to shoot the Union's wooden warships to pieces. But how could they make an ironclad warship without a shipyard?

The state of Virginia left the Union and joined the Confederate States in 1861. The Union's shipyard in Portsmouth, Virginia, was suddenly in Southern hands. The Union soldiers there had to flee as the Confederates came in, but as they left they destroyed as much as they could.

The South now had a shipyard. Confederate shipbuilders came in and found that the North had accidentally left them what they needed to begin building an ironclad.

The *Merrimack* had been at the shipyard for repairs when the North fled. It was one of the Union navy's biggest and most powerful warships.

The Union didn't want to leave the *Merrimack* for the Confederates, so they burned it as they were leaving.

In their rush to leave, the Union didn't completely destroy the ship. It sank in the shallow river, and the fire burned only down to the waterline.

The Confederates brought up what was left of the *Merrimack* and found that the engines and the bottom part of the hull were still usable.

Confederate shipbuilders built their ironclad on top of what was left of the *Merrimack*.

The Confederates had big hopes for their untested new ship. The thick iron armor would protect her from cannonballs and shells. She could destroy the Union warships near Norfolk and then steam up the Potomac River and bomb Washington, D.C.

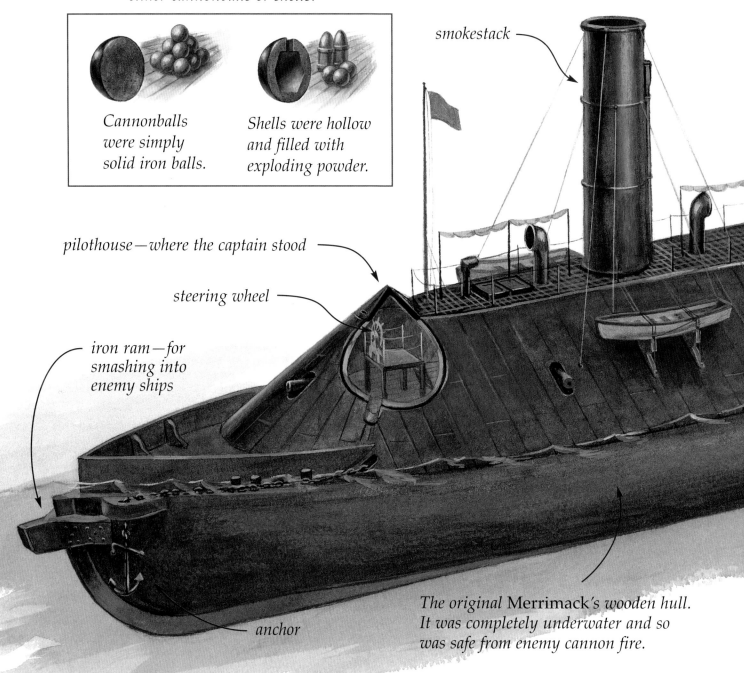

Ships' cannons could fire either cannonballs or shells.

Cannonballs were simply solid iron balls.

Shells were hollow and filled with exploding powder.

smokestack

pilothouse—where the captain stood

steering wheel

iron ram—for smashing into enemy ships

anchor

The original Merrimack's *wooden hull. It was completely underwater and so was safe from enemy cannon fire.*

No one knows exactly how the inside of the Virginia *was laid out.*

The Confederates named their new ironclad the *Virginia*, but Northerners called it by its earlier name, the *Merrimack*. Many people today still call the *Virginia* the *Merrimack*.

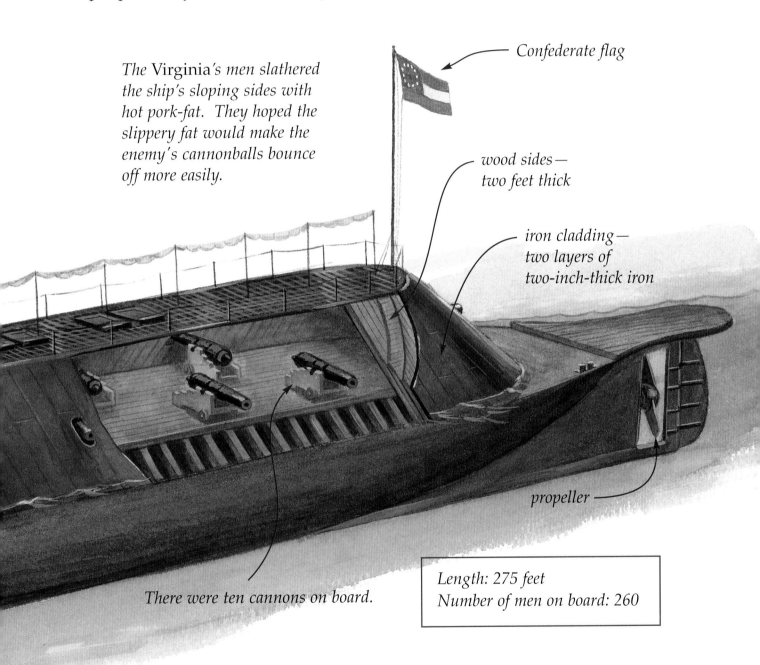

The Virginia*'s men slathered the ship's sloping sides with hot pork-fat. They hoped the slippery fat would make the enemy's cannonballs bounce off more easily.*

Confederate flag

wood sides— two feet thick

iron cladding— two layers of two-inch-thick iron

propeller

There were ten cannons on board.

Length: 275 feet
Number of men on board: 260

Spies for the Union had been watching the construction of the strange new ship. Before it was finished they sneaked up to Washington and told the Union navy about it. The navy started to get worried. They needed their own ironclad, and they needed it fast.

The Union turned to an inventor named John Ericsson. He had an idea for an ironclad warship that was completely different from any ship ever made. He brought his designs to Washington and met with the men in charge of the navy. They were not sure what to think about the inventor's strange design.

However, President Lincoln liked the idea, so the navy asked Ericsson to build his ironclad. The Confederates' ironclad in Virginia was almost complete after about three months of construction. If the North didn't have their own ironclad in time, the South's new ship would be unstoppable. It was a race to finish building first, and the South was already way ahead before the North had even begun.

Ericsson rushed
back to New York and got
started. When the ship was
being built in Brooklyn, New York, many people said it would sink
like a stone. It didn't even look like a ship. Where were the sails?
And why were there only two cannons?

But Ericsson was so sure of his ironclad that he rode on the deck as
it splashed into the water for the first time.

Ericsson did not even call his creation a ship—he called it a fighting
machine. He named his new machine the *Monitor*.

From the propeller and the anchor to the engines and the cannons, Ericsson personally designed everything on the *Monitor*. He even invented the first flushing toilets on a ship.

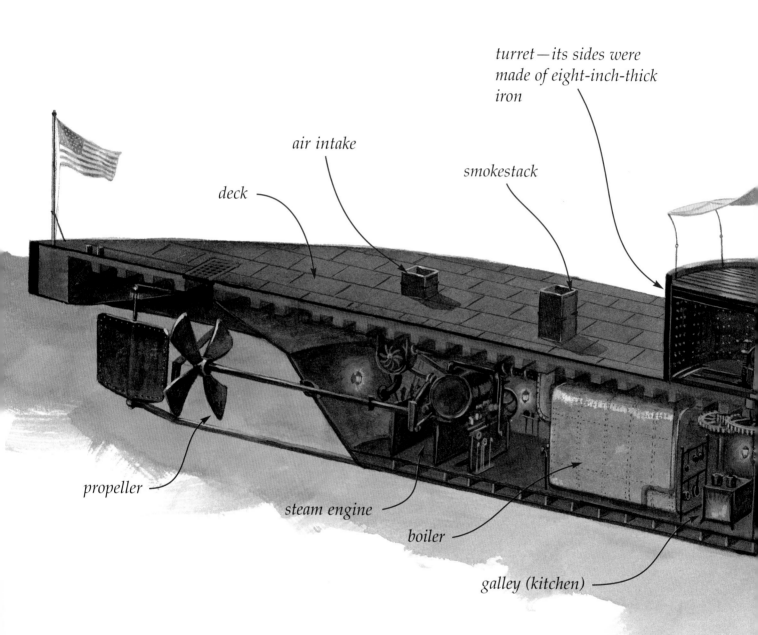

turret—*its sides were made of eight-inch-thick iron*

air intake

smokestack

deck

propeller

steam engine

boiler

galley (kitchen)

Before battle, the air intakes, smokestacks, and awnings were taken down. This left only the turret and pilothouse on the deck, which was only about eighteen inches above the waterline. The rest of the ship was underwater. The enemy would not have much to shoot at.

Ericsson's most important innovation was the revolving turret. On all other warships, including the new *Virginia*, the cannons faced outward and could not be turned. They could fire at an enemy only when the whole ship was turned in the right direction. But the *Monitor*'s two cannons were in a turret that revolved, so the cannons could fire in any direction just by turning the turret.

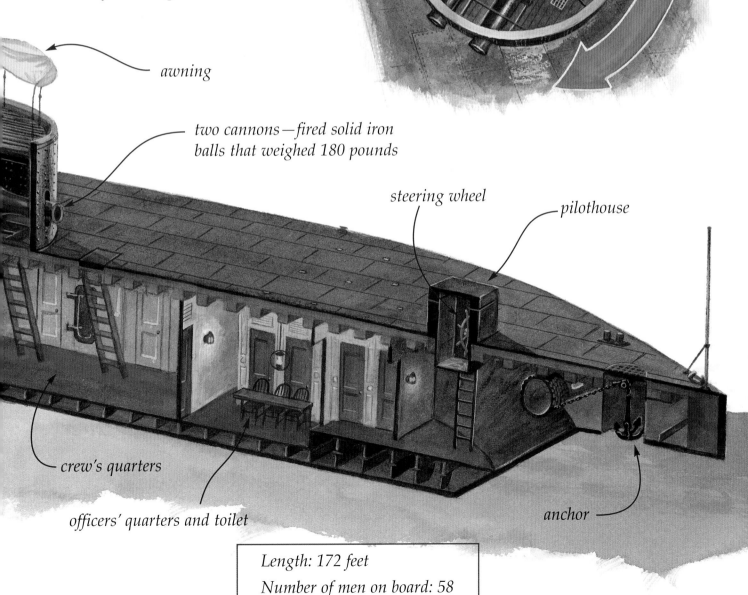

awning

two cannons—fired solid iron balls that weighed 180 pounds

steering wheel

pilothouse

crew's quarters

officers' quarters and toilet

anchor

Length: 172 feet
Number of men on board: 58

The *Monitor* was designed and built in only 100 days. When she was completed there was little time for testing. Spies had told the North that the South's big ironclad was just about finished and would soon begin attacking the North's wooden warships. So on March 6, 1862, the *Monitor* was towed out of New York harbor and down the Atlantic coast toward Virginia.

On the morning of the second day at sea the *Monitor* was hit by a violent storm. The ironclad rode so low in the water that the waves washed over the whole deck. Seawater poured into the ship from the base of the turret like a waterfall. The men desperately pumped out the water to keep the ship from going down.

When the *Monitor* reached the shores of Virginia, the men could hear the distant booming of cannon fire across the water. As the evening darkened, the captain, John Worden, watched the bright orange glow of a burning ship on the horizon. Were they too late?

While the *Monitor* was being built, the Southerners had raced to complete the *Virginia*. Their spies had told them that the North's ironclad was taking shape with amazing speed. The *Virginia*'s captain, Franklin Buchanan, was in a hurry to get his ironclad into action, so on the morning of March 8 he sent the shipbuilders ashore before the ship was quite finished and steamed out to meet the enemy.

The Union ships were in Hampton Roads, an area of water in Virginia where the James and the Elizabeth Rivers come together and flow into the Chesapeake Bay.

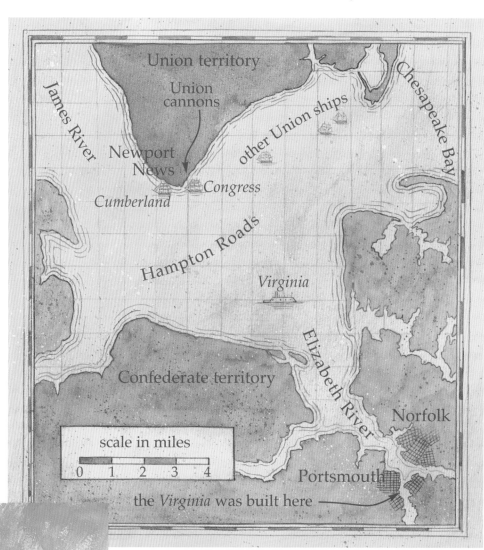

Captain Buchanan quickly found that his new ironclad was sluggish and hard to steer. But he trusted the iron armor to protect the ship from all enemy fire. He took the *Virginia* into battle on its very first cruise.

Buchanan steered the *Virginia* straight for the USS *Cumberland*, a warship with twenty-four cannons. The *Cumberland* fired on the *Virginia*, but the shell bounced harmlessly off the ironclad's sloping iron sides. Union ships and the cannons onshore opened up with everything they had, smashing the *Virginia* with enough firepower to blow any other ship out of the water. But the *Virginia* kept on coming.

The *Virginia* rammed into the side of the *Cumberland*, driving her bow deep into the Union ship's wooden hull. The *Cumberland* began to fill with water and sink, but the *Virginia*'s ram was stuck in its side. Buchanan ordered the engines to full-speed reverse. With her propeller churning the muddy water, the *Virginia* finally pulled free. The *Cumberland*'s men continued blasting the *Virginia*'s iron sides with cannon fire as their ship slowly sank into the shallow river.

Buchanan then turned his ironclad toward the USS *Congress*, a ship with fifty cannons. He knew that his own brother was an officer on the *Congress*, but he was still determined to destroy the enemy ship.

The *Congress*'s captain saw what had happened to the *Cumberland*, so he desperately steered for the shallow water near shore and purposely grounded his ship. He was stuck in the mud, but he knew that the *Virginia* sat deep in the water and could not get close without also getting stuck. The *Virginia* simply stayed in the deeper water and blasted the *Congress* with cannon fire until the Union ship surrendered.

Even though the Union ship had surrendered, the Union cannons onshore continued to fire. This made Captain Buchanan so angry that he ordered his men to burn the *Congress*. Then he climbed out to the open top deck of the *Virginia* and fired his rifle at the shore. A Union bullet tore into his leg, and he was carried below. Lieutenant Catesby Jones was made captain of the ship.

The *Virginia*'s men set fire to the *Congress* after letting most of the Union men, including Buchanan's brother, escape to safety. With evening coming on and the tide going out, Jones steered the *Virginia* back to the southern shore, determined to return the next morning and finish off the rest of the Union warships. He didn't know that the *Monitor* was rushing to the scene and would arrive later that night.

Still ten miles away, the *Monitor*'s captain Worden watched the orange glow of the burning *Congress* and hoped he wasn't too late.

Telegraphs were sent to Washington describing the disastrous battle. Nearly 300 Union sailors had been killed. President Lincoln called an emergency meeting. The secretary of war was so alarmed that he sent telegraphs to Northern cities along the coast saying, "Man your guns. Block your harbors. The *Merrimack* is coming."

Northerners either didn't know or didn't care that the South had given the old *Merrimack* a new name.

When the *Monitor* finally steamed into Hampton Roads that night, the Union fleet was in a panic. The appearance of the little *Monitor*, with only two cannons on board, didn't make anyone feel any better. Was this strange little ship supposed to save them from the South's iron monster?

Early the next morning, March 9, 1862, the *Virginia* steamed back into Hampton Roads, expecting to finish off the rest of the Union warships. But peering out of the pilothouse, Captain Jones saw something strange floating low in the water, blocking his path—it was the *Monitor*.

Captain Jones gave the order, and the *Virginia*'s cannons roared. The shells exploded against the *Monitor*'s turret. The *Monitor* returned fire, and her shots slammed into the *Virginia*'s sloping iron sides. The first

Thousands of people watched from the shores as the ironclads pounded away at each other. The smaller, faster *Monitor* circled the slow, hulking *Virginia*, searching for a weakness.

The *Virginia*'s captain tried to ram the *Monitor*. He steamed slowly toward his enemy, but the *Monitor* turned away at the last moment. The two ironclads scraped together, cannons blazing at each other from only a few feet away.

On the *Virginia*, almost everything outside of the armor was blasted away. But the heavy iron plates on the ship's sloping sides kept the men inside safe. Peering through the gun ports, the men fired their cannons when the *Monitor* came in sight.

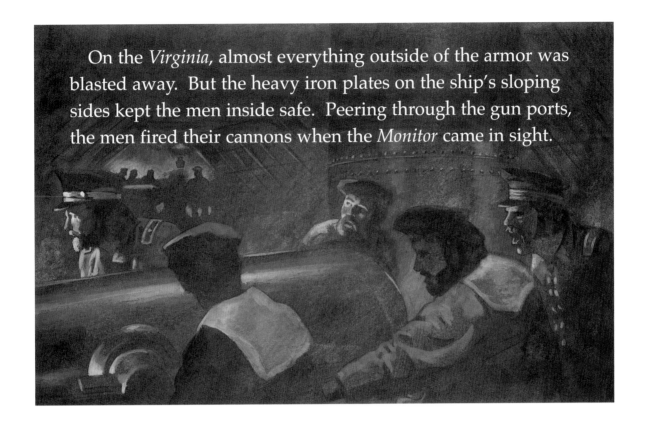

Inside the *Monitor*, the men found that the revolving turret was difficult to get moving. Once it was turning, however, it was difficult to stop. So they turned the cannon ports away from the *Virginia* to load the cannons. Then they started the turret turning and fired as the cannons swung around toward the *Virginia*.

The noise in the turret was deafening with the roar of the cannons on the inside and shells from the Virginia *hammering on the outside.*

Captain Worden was standing in the *Monitor's* pilothouse watching through the small eye slit. Suddenly a shell from the *Virginia* exploded against the pilothouse. Worden was temporarily blinded by the blast and had to be carried below.

In the confusion that followed the wounding of the captain, the *Monitor* moved away from the battle. The *Virginia*'s captain assumed that the *Monitor* had given up, so he turned his ship back to port. After four hours, the duel of the ironclads was over.

The battle was a draw. But even though neither ship had won, they had fought one of the most important sea battles in history. Each ship had been hit with enough firepower to smash any wooden warship to pieces. Everyone could see that all the navies of the world were suddenly out-of-date. The mighty wooden sailing ships with their rows and rows of heavy cannons could easily be destroyed by a small iron-armored ship. From then on, iron warships would rule the seas.

After the success of the *Monitor*, inventor John Ericsson and others were kept busy building new, improved ironclads for the Union.

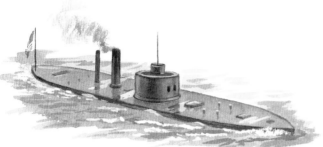

The Onondaga—*a monitor with two turrets. The U.S. Navy built thirty-five monitors during the Civil War*

The Passaic—*this kind of ship came to be known as a monitor*

The New Ironsides

A "Pook turtle"—named after the designer, Samuel Pook

The South also built more ironclads:

The Tennessee

The Manassas—*a strange egg-shaped craft with one cannon*

The Albemarle

The *Monitor* and the *Virginia* never met again in battle. Neither of the famous dueling ironclads lasted for more than a year.

The *Virginia* had survived the Union's cannons, but her own men destroyed her in the end. The Confederates were forced to flee from the navy yard when Union soldiers stormed into Norfolk in May of 1862. The Southerners didn't want to leave their *Virginia* to the Union forces, so before they left, they set fire to their beloved ironclad. When the fire reached the gunpowder on board, a huge explosion destroyed the ship.

The *Monitor* was no longer needed in Virginia, so Union leaders decided to tow the ship down the Atlantic coast to North Carolina to help the Union navy there.

The *Monitor* was hit by a violent storm off the coast of Cape Hatteras on the night of December 30, 1862. The small, low ironclad was designed for the calm waters of rivers and harbors, not the heavy seas of the Atlantic Ocean. In an area known as "the graveyard of the Atlantic," the *Monitor* sank to its final resting place at the bottom of the ocean.

AFTERWORD

Sixteen miles off Cape Hatteras, North Carolina, the *Monitor* lies upside down on the sandy seafloor. The ship had rolled over as it fell through the water. The turret separated from the hull on the way down and hit bottom first. Then the hull fell on top of it.

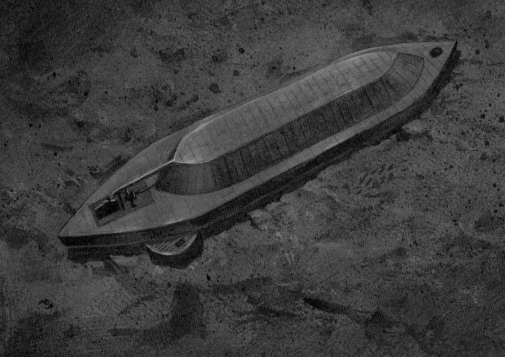

Marine archaeologists found the *Monitor* in 1973, and the U.S. government designated the wreck site as the Monitor National Marine Sanctuary. The iron ship was decaying badly, but divers managed to bring up some parts of the wreck. For more than a hundred years the *Monitor* had been lost at the bottom of the sea. Now pieces of the historic ironclad, including the famous turret, can be seen at the Mariners' Museum in Newport News, Virginia. The rest of the historic iron ship still lies 240 feet beneath the waves, a ghostly memorial to the *Monitor*, the *Virginia*, and the duel of the ironclads.